# MY BOOK OF CHRISTMAS CAROLS

A Platt & Munk ALL ABOARD BOOK™

# MY BOOK OF
## CHRISTMAS CAROLS

### Collected by B. Rosenkrans
### Illustrated by Jane Dyer

**Platt & Munk, Publishers**

Copyright © 1986 by Platt & Munk, Publishers, a division of Grosset & Dunlap. Illustrations copyright © 1986 by Jane Dyer. All rights reserved. Grosset & Dunlap is a member of The Putnam Publishing Group, New York. ALL ABOARD BOOKS is a trademark of The Putnam Publishing Group. Published simultaneously in Canada. Printed in the U.S.A. Library of Congress Catalog Card Number: 86-80290 ISBN 0-448-19079-6

A B C D E F G H I J

# O COME, ALL YE FAITHFUL
## (ADESTE FIDELIS)

Probably dating from the seventeenth century, this hymn was sung in Latin for
many, many years. Translated into English in the last century,
it is still often heard in the Latin original.

**English trans. by Rev. Frederick Oakeley, 1841**

*With dignity*

O come, all ye faith-ful, Joy-ful and tri - um - phant, O come ye, O
Sing, choirs of an - gels, Sing in ex - ul - ta - tion, O sing, all ye

come ye to Beth - le - hem, Come and be - hold Him,
ci - ti - zens of heav - en a - bove; Glo - ry to God, All

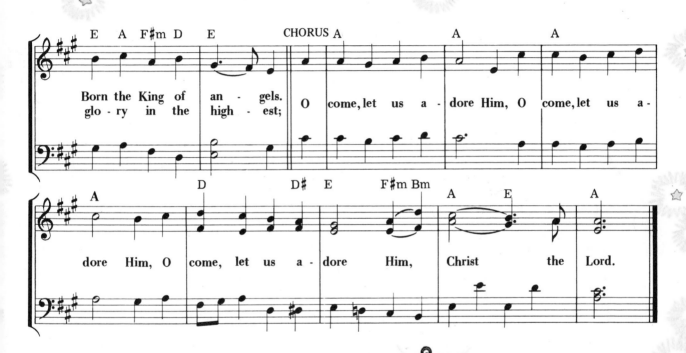

Born the King of an - gels.
glo - ry in the high - est;
O come, let us a - dore Him, O come, let us a -
dore Him, O come, let us a - dore Him, Christ the Lord.

Yea, Lord, we greet Thee,
Born this happy morning,
Jesus, to Thee be glory given;
Word of the Father,
Now in flesh appearing:
  CHORUS

*Adeste fideles, lacti triumphantes,*
*Venite, venite in Bethlehem;*
*Natum videte, Regem angelorum:*
*Venite adoremus,*
*Venite adoremus,*
*Venite adoremus,*
*Dominum.*

# JOY TO THE WORLD!

The great English theologian and hymnist, Isaac Watts,
based this hymn on the 98th psalm of the Old Testament.

Isaac Watts, 1719

Anonymous

He rules the world with truth and grace,
And makes the nations prove
The glories of His righteousness,
And wonders of His love,
And wonders of His love,
And wonders, and wonders of His love.

# IT CAME UPON A MIDNIGHT CLEAR

Both the words and music of this nineteenth century carol are American.

Edmund H. Sears, 1850

Richard S. Willis, 1850

It came up-on a mid-night clear, That glo-ious song of
Still through the clo-ven skies they come, With peace-ful wings un-

old, From an-gels bend-ing near the earth, To touch their harps of gold: "Peace
furl'd, And still their heav'n-ly mu-sic floats O'er all the wea-ry world; A-

on the earth, good will to men From heav'n's all gra-cious King." The
bove its sad and low-ly plains They bend on hov-'ring wing, And

world in sol-emn still-ness lay To hear the an-gels sing.
ev-er o'er its ba-bel sounds The bless-ed an-gels sing.

8

For lo! the days are hast'ning on,
By prophets seen of old,
When with the ever circling years
Shall come the time foretold,
When the new heav'n and earth shall own
The Prince of Peace their King,
And the whole world send back the song
Which now the angels sing.

# AWAY IN A MANGER

A sweet hymn once attributed to Martin Luther,
the song was long referred to as "Luther's Cradle Hymn."
However, it is more probably a nineteenth century American lullaby.

*Sweetly*

A - way in a man - ger, No crib for a bed, The lit - tle Lord
The cat - tle are low - ing, The poor Ba - by wakes, But lit - tle Lord

Je - sus Laid down His sweet head, The stars in the sky Looked
Je - sus, No cry - ing He makes, I love Thee, Lord Je - sus, Look

down where He lay, The lit - tle Lord Je - sus A - sleep on the hay.
down from the sky, And stay by my cra - dle Till morn - ing is nigh.

Be near me, Lord Jesus,
I ask Thee to stay
Close by me forever,
And love me, I pray;

Bless all the dear children
In Thy tender care,
And take us to heaven,
To live with Thee there.

# DECK THE HALLS

A particularly joyous song, "Deck the Halls" is a traditional Welsh carol.

Deck the halls with boughs of hol - ly,
See the blaz - ing Yule be - fore us,
Fa la la la la, la la la la.

'Tis the sea - son to be jol - ly,
Strike the harp and join the cho - rus,
Fa la la la la, la la la la.

Don we now our gay ap - par - el,
Fol - low me in mer - ry meas - ure,
Fa la la la la la la la la.

Troll the an - cient Yule - tide car - ol,
While I tell of Yule - tide treas - ure,
Fa la la la la, la la la la.

Fast away the old year passes,
Fa la la la la, la la la la.
Hail the new, ye lads and lasses,
Fa la la la la, la la la la.
Sing we joyous all together,
Fa la la, la la la, la la la,
Heedless of the wind and weather,
Fa la la la la, la la la la.

# O LITTLE TOWN OF BETHLEHEM

An American carol, it is thought to have been written on Christmas Eve by a clergyman named Phillips Brooks and set to music by Lewis Redner, the church organist.

**Phillips Brooks, 1868**

**Lewis H. Redner, 1868**

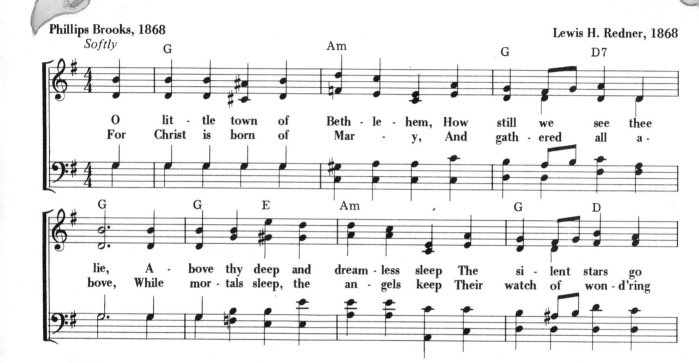

O lit - tle town of Beth - le - hem, How still we see thee
For Christ is born of Mar - y, And gath - ered all a -

lie, A - bove thy deep and dream - less sleep The si - lent stars go
bove, While mor - tals sleep, the an - gels keep Their watch of won - d'ring

14

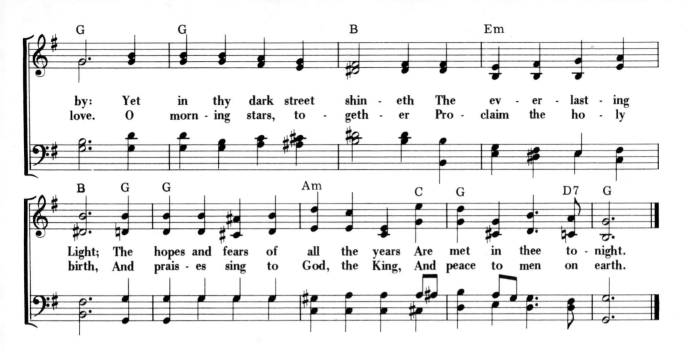

by: Yet in thy dark street shin - eth The ev - er - last - ing
love. O morn - ing stars, to - geth - er Pro - claim the ho - ly

Light; The hopes and fears of all the years Are met in thee to - night.
birth, And prais - es sing to God, the King, And peace to men on earth.

O holy Child of Bethlehem,
Descend to us, we pray;
Cast out our sin, and enter in,
Be born in us today.
We hear the Christmas angels
The great glad tidings tell;
O come to us, abide with us,
Our Lord Emmanuel.

How silently, how silently,
The wondrous gift is given;
So God imparts to human hearts
The blessing of His heaven.
No ear may hear His coming,
But in this world of sin,
Where meek souls will receive Him still,
The dear Christ enters in.

# THE COVENTRY CAROL

This old English lullaby-carol is thought to have been used originally
as part of a medieval Christmas pageant held in the town of Coventry.

O sisters, too, how may we do,
For to preserve this day;
This poor Youngling for whom we sing,
Bye, bye, lully, lullay.

Herod the King, in his raging,
Charged he hath this day
His men of might, in his own sight,
All children young to slay.

Then woe is me, poor Child, for thee,
And ever mourn and say,
For thy parting nor say nor sing,
Bye, bye, lully, lullay.

# HARK! THE HERALD ANGELS SING

A glorious hymn, it is one of the most popular of several thousand written
by the famous English evangelist Charles Wesley.

Charles Wesley (1707-1788)

Felix Mendelssohn, 1840
Arranged by W.H. Cummings, 1855

*Joyfully*

Hark! the her - ald an - gels sing, ___ "Glo - ry to the new - born King!
Christ by high - est heav'n a - dored; ___ Christ the ev - er - last - ing Lord;

Peace on earth, and mer - cy mild, ___ God and sin - ners rec - on - ciled."
Late in time be - hold Him come, ___ Off - spring of the fa - vored one.

Joy - ful, all ye na - tions, rise, Join the tri - umph of the skies; ___
Veiled in flesh, the God - head see; Hail th'in - car - nate De - i - ty, ___

18

With th'an - gel - ic host pro - claim, "Christ is born in Beth - le - hem."
Pleased as man with men to dwell, Je - sus our Im - man - u - el!

CHORUS

Hark! the her - ald an - gels sing, "Glo - ry to the new - born King!"

Hail! the heav'n-born Prince of Peace!
Hail! the Son of Righteousness!
Light and life to all He brings,
Ris'n with healing in His wings.
Mild He lays His glory by,
Born that man no more may die,
Born to raise the sons of earth,
Born to give them second birth.
*CHORUS*

19

# JINGLE BELLS

A popular Christmas song for over a century, "Jingle Bells"
was originally known as "The One-horse Open Sleigh."

**Words and music by
John Pierpont, 1857**

*Brightly*

Dash - ing through the snow in a one - horse o - pen sleigh,
A day or two a - go I thought I'd take a ride,

O'er the fields we go, laugh - ing all the way;
And soon Miss Fan - nie Bright was seat - ed by my side.

Bells on bob - tail ring, mak - ing spir - its bright; What
The horse was lean and lank; Mis - for - tune seemed his lot; He

fun it is to ride and sing a sleigh - ing song to - night! } Oh,
got in - to a drift - ed bank And we, we got up - sot.

# THE FIRST NOEL

"The First Noel" is an old folk carol which may have originated in France.

el, Born is the King of Is - ra - el.

And by the light of that same star,
Three wise men came from country far,
To seek for a King was their intent,
And to follow the star wherever it went.
CHORUS

This star drew nigh to the northwest,
Over Bethlehem it took its rest,
And there it did both stop and stay
Right over the place where Jesus lay.
CHORUS

# WE THREE KINGS OF ORIENT ARE

In this nineteenth century American carol, each of the three kings
tells of the gift he brought to the baby, Jesus.

Words and music by
Rev. John H. Hopkins, Jr.

We three kings of O-ri-ent are, Bear-ing gifts we trav-erse far, Field and foun-tain, moor and moun-tain, Fol-low-ing yon-der Star.

**CHORUS**

O star of won-der, star of might, Star with roy-al beau-ty bright,

West-ward lead-ing, still pro-ceed-ing, Guide us to the per-fect light.

24

*Gaspar*:
Born a king on Bethlehem's plain,
Gold I bring to crown Him again;
King forever, ceasing never,
Over us all to reign.
CHORUS

*Melchior*:
Frankincense to offer have I,
Incense owns a Deity nigh,
Pray'r and praising, all men raising,
Worship Him, God on high.
CHORUS

*Balthasar*:
Myrrh is mine; its bitter perfume
Breathes a life of gath'ring gloom;
Sorrowing, sighing, bleeding, dying,
Sealed in the stone-cold tomb.
CHORUS

Glorious now behold Him arise,
King and God and Sacrifice;
Alleluia, Alleluia,
Earth to the heav'ns replies.
CHORUS

25

# WHAT CHILD IS THIS?

The melody for this carol is also known as "Greensleeves." It dates from at least the sixteenth century, although the tune was not used as the basis for a Christmas carol until much later.

**William C. Dix (1837-1898)**

**Old English air**
**Arranged by Sir John Stainer**

# ANGELS WE HAVE HEARD ON HIGH

Also called the "Angel's Hymn," the carol is sung to an old
French melody and is considered to be one of the first Christmas hymns.

*With spirit*

An - gels we have heard on high, Sweet - ly sing - ing o'er the plains;

And the moun - tains in re - ply, Ech - o - ing their joy - ous strains.

CHORUS

Glo - - - - - - - - ri - a

in ex - cel - sis De - o Glo - - -

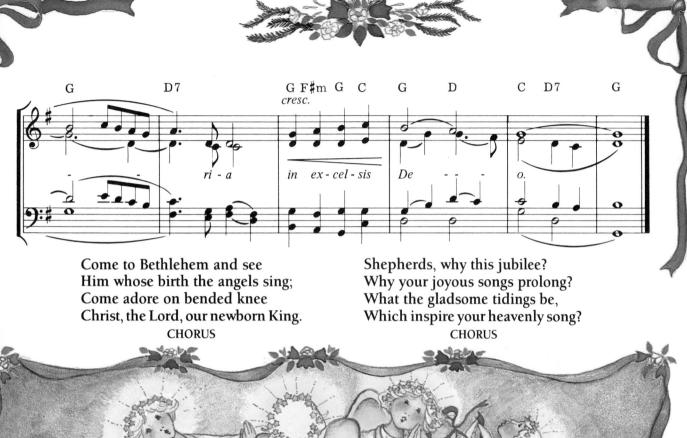

Come to Bethlehem and see
Him whose birth the angels sing;
Come adore on bended knee
Christ, the Lord, our newborn King.
CHORUS

Shepherds, why this jubilee?
Why your joyous songs prolong?
What the gladsome tidings be,
Which inspire your heavenly song?
CHORUS

# SILENT NIGHT

This well-loved Austrian carol was written on Christmas Eve, 1818.

Joseph Möhr, 1818

Franz Xavier Grüber, 1818

*Slowly and softly*

Si - lent night, Ho - ly night! All is calm, all is bright,

'Round yon Vir - gin Moth - er and Child, Ho - ly In - fant so ten - der and mild,

Sleep in heav - en - ly peace, Sleep in heav - en - ly peace.

Silent night, Holy night!
Shepherds quake at the sight!
Glories stream from heaven afar,
Heav'nly hosts sing, "Alleluia!"
Christ, the Savior, is born,
Christ, the Savior, is born.

Silent night, Holy night!
Son of God, love's pure light,
Radiant beams from Thy Holy face,
With the dawn of redeeming grace,
Jesus, Lord, at Thy birth,
Jesus, Lord, at Thy birth.

31

# INDEX OF CHRISTMAS CAROLS